THE ART OF COMMUNICATION

INZEMAM ALAM

Contents

Foreword

In this modern age, communication is one skill that a person requires most. No matter what job a person is doing, what field he is in, whether a student or an job person everyone will require communication skills. You will have to use these skills no matter where you are. You need them to talk to your client, you need them to talk to give presentation, or any school project. This book contains some basic ideas behind communication. The pillars on which communication skills are build. It also tells on how to improve and build those pillars so that your skills are build strong from its foundation. Hope this book helps you develop or improve your communication skills.

Acknowledgements

Firstly, I would like to thank Allah (The Most Merciful) without whose wish nothing was possible.

I would like to thank ***Dr. Habiba Kausar****, my sister who helped me as editor. I would like to thank my parents (Er. Aftab Alam and Zahida Aftab) who provided me with all the sources required. I would like to thank my Brother Intekhab Alam for his invaluable motivation.*

I would like to thank Notion Press for approaching and providing me this opportunity for publishing this book.

1

What is Communication?

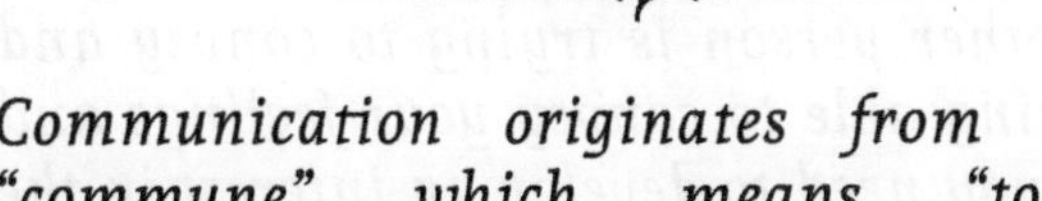

Communication originates from the word "commune" which means "to share". Communication is the art of sharing information, feelings etc to a person or group of person without letting the loose interest. So basically, communication isn't talking or holding conversation, it is a much deeper concept. In layman language one can say that communication is sharing your experience with someone without annoying them.

In order to have a good communication skill one needs to learn to be silent. Consider a person who has good command over english language and has a nice level of confidence but he doesn't like to listen, in that case we cannot say that his communication skills are good. Having a good communication skills means analysing the situation at hand and thinking of all the possible reaction that can be given and then choosing the best or close to best option. If a person can do this automatically then we can say that his communication skill are top level. In order to do so one needs to analyse situation which can be done only by staying silent when needed and listening to the conversation,facts etc. For good communication one needs to understand the motive that stands behind the whole topic, the mindset of the person you are holding conversation with. A good communication skill is when you are able to feel what the other person is trying to convey and not just being able to convey your feelings and to do that you need to develop an interest in the conversation.

Let us take an example, suppose that you are doing some work on your computer and then somone enters the room and is saying something to you, at that point your entire focus is on your work and your least interested in his/ her words but suddenly they say that your crush was asking about you. Your entire attention shifts to that person, you listen to them carefully, there every single word, this is because now you have interest. Therefore, interest is necessary to have good communication skill.

To develop interest in every single conversation one needs to have learning approach in life. He should see everyone whether younger or older with a view that there might be something that he can learn something from them. When a person has this type of approach this when they truly grow in life. A growth is when a person is continously learning from his surrounding. That type of man is truly successful because he/ she may fail once or twice or more time but they will learn from it and because of that they will avoid failing many more times.

ᑭᑭᑭ

Self-Notes

2
Parts of Communication Skills

To build a good communication skills one needs to first understand where he/she is lacking. They need to understand where they are lacking and then work on each area one by one. One might say they can speak confidently but cannot wait to listen to others thoughts completely, other might say they listen and talk confidently but still they somehow offend others. So in order to be a good communicator one needs to work on different areas one by one.

At the very basic one needs to start listening because listening is the basic foundation of every other aspect. Listening is not just waiting for your turn to come. It is the total process of hearing what the other person is saying with interest and try to understand his/her feelings during the conversation. Listening is very important to understand the situation and then reacting accordingly. When you have good listening skills people often tend to talk more to you. They like talking to you since you listen them, carefully, which is a major feat in communication skills.

There are few ways given which can eventually help you to become a good listener.

Have a learning approach: A learning approach will help you develop an honest interest in the conversation. Showing an interest in what the other person is saying will help you in many ways. It will help you in better understanding of the situation which eventually lead to better replies from you.

Do not jump to conclusion: If someone is telling you their problems or something that happened with them, don't directly jump to conclusion.

For example, something happened to him/her because he/she did this or they should have done this.

This type of approach usually make you seem like nosy and people tend to get more angry.

Do not give unasked advice: Giving advice when it is not asked can make the other person irritated by you. Even if you have gone through same problem giving advice when uncalled for is not a good communication skill. One might have an entirely different approach, perspective to that problem and your advice may offend him and even be useless to him.

Let them burn the steam: Sometimes all you need to do is stay silent and let them pour out all their feelings. Understanding when you need to stay silent and let them burn their stem is a sign of good communication skill.

You need to be an inclusive communicator. An inclusive communicator means one which takes care not to offend other people with their personal views. If the opposite happens then the conversation shifts to one side. At that point the other person starts avoiding talking to you because you tend to dominate their views without any consideration. You need to avoid communicating in a way that will eventually pressurise your views, opinions on others. To do that you need to understand the mindset of other people and that is done by keen observation.

Observation is not just simply looking at something carefully. It is the process in which you silently understand the situation, grasping every single loose end of the conversation and then control it as you like. It is quite more difficult than it seems. Because here you don't have to do anything which is much tougher than it looks. You need to stay quite then listen to the other person, try to understand his position while they are talking and then understanding their feeling and choose the best option for your reply which will convey your words without offending them. While in a conversation try to grasp situation while someone is speaking and then take a pause to recollect your thoughts and then answer accordingly. It's just like when you are attacked on a castle after defending you look at your army and decide the best move to make the best damage.

Sometimes you may come across people who are not that easy to understand. In that case you can ask a few questions related to things they told you about and then slowly gather clues and understand their mindset.

For example, suppose that you are a sales representative and you need to meet a client. Now there are numerous schemes available of a certain investment plan but you now don't know which scheme you might persuade them to. One might be too expensive for them and they will move out immediately while the other becomes inexpensive that there could be your loss. At that point you can start talking about the company and investments in general, then the response form the client may help you in gauging the amount they can spend. If it still doesn't work you can start asking questions about their job or education and interactively tell them about yours just so that they don't get uncomfortable with all your questions. After all this you will have an idea of their mentality, their expenditures etc. and now you can select a few schemes which are neither too expensive nor too cheap. In this way few questions can help you in understanding your clients mindset.

While this may apply to normal conversation it does not hold true for all type of conversation like an argumentative one. In an argumentative one you need to deal with more patience or else the arguments will never end. You might need to take some steps back and then reconsider your and their position and then act accordingly. Reconsidering your thoughts might even widen your views that eventually you might find some flaws or some truth in their points. Sometimes you might have to agree with the other person for the sake of avoiding arguments.

For example, you are working on a piece of document and someone starts taking out faults even though there is none but then you have to act patiently and agree to them a little to avoid baseless arguments. In that case you can use small questions like "Oh I see, it would be helpful if you tell me how to correct these" to turn the conversation in a different direction.

Now another very important thing for communication is to build one. It means that from a very small statement you start to build an entire conversation. This is very helpful in case you want to attract some clients to you. To do so first you need to understand the concept of close and open ended question.

Close ended question means a question is asked and answer is given and that conversation ends right there.

For example, your friend says to you that he is going to someplace for vacation and you answer "wonderful, have fun". At that point the conversation ends immidiately right after replying to that question.

Open ended question are ones in which one question leads to another and in this manner one big conversation is held.

In the same above example if instead of replying "wonderful, have fun" you start asking question about the trip it will lead to an entire conversation which could even change it's course.

So with open ended question you can actually build a conversation and also control it accordingly. So in this way you will be available to build and control conversation which quite necesary if you are in field where you need to do a lot of conversation with clients or your colleagues or boss.

While holding a conversation there are certain things that are to be avoided.

1. *Gossip: One needs to avoid gossiping about other persons. Even the person to whom you are gossiping to will also avoid talking to you because he will think that you are gossiping about him also. So gossiping in no way will benefit you.*

2. *Judging: You shouldn't be judging other people on the basis of their behaviour or their conversation. People will start avoiding you if you keep judging them. According to them sharing anything with you is a disadvantage because you will judge them.*

3. *Negativity: A negative approach in life will eventually make you to depressed and will also make anyone talking to you depressed. People will eventually start avoiding you because of your negative approach towards everything. Keeping a negative aspect of things in mind is okay, but to actually make that negativity your attitude will never get you anywhere.*

4.

Complaining: In life there are many problems and hardship, but complaining about every small thing is just irritating. Whenever a person starts talking to you all you do is complaint about this and that. Eventually people will get too irritated from you.

5.

Lying: I believe i don't need to explain what this means and why to avoid this. Ofcourse no one prefers to talk to someone of whom we don't know whether it's true or not.

6.

Exxageration: Exxageration is one thing which a person mostly does withou knowing. One needs to understand that there might be something which makes him too much happy but it is not an item of that much exxageration. One needs to understand its true value or else everything will be exxagerated and whene you talk to the person they will not be able to understand whether it is that good for real or you are exaagerating out of habit.

7.

Excuses: You need to stop making excuses for anything if you do. Blame game is not a good habit. It will eventually make people irritated from hearing your excuses and blames.

8.

Dogmatism: Dogmatism is when you lay down your opinion as fact. It's like imposing your views on others like they are true and fact irrespective of the fact that they could be false. Forcing you views on others will do you no good while communicating. You need to calmly without presuarising palce your opinion and try to understand their mindset and opinion too.

These were things to be avoided and there are few things that will surely help you in better communicating.

1. *Honesty: Just be honest. Most people don't react much with your views or anything. In fact, they might like talking to you since you always speak honestly.*

2. *Authenticity: Just be yourself. No matter how perfect you are at faking but in face to face conversation you might let some clue down hinting that you are faking. Once that happens people loose interest in communicating with you. So be yourself. Put forth the ideas, opinions and views that you*

actually have. But remember not to force them on others.

3.

Integrity: Be on your word. If you have said something to someone then be on it even if you talk to another person. People often tend to like person who keep their words.

4.

Love: Not in a romantic way, it means a happy, caring feeling. Like greeting them with a smile, talking politely, listening to them calmly and wishing them well.

5.

Body Language: Your body language speaks louder than your voice. Keep in mind to keep your body in way that shows confidence anddoen not look alarming to others. For example,

- *Keeping your back straight will show more confidence.*
- *Using your hand a little bit while talking shows interest and interactiveness.*
-

While you are talking to someone avoid keeping your hand in pocket because it shows presence of attitude and the view that you think you are not much interested.

- *Show a little facial expression like smiling, controlling your eyes a little to show you are interested in conversation.*

- *Making direct eye contact shows presence of confidence.*

- *If you are seated, then avoid crossing legs since it shows a sense of superiority.*

- *If you are seated, you might shake legs or continously keep tapping it on ground, avoid doing so because it is a clear indicator of nervousness which is not good while communicating.*

- *Keep an open body posture instead of a shrinking one (like you are freezing) it shows that you are open to socialise.*

- *Keep you muscles relaxed not stiff or else it will show that you are uncomfortable in the conversation.*

•

Try to maintain your original relaxed position to show that you are completely comfortable.

ÞÞÞ

Self-Notes

3

Few Important Things

Inclusive Communicator

An inclusive communicator means one which takes care not to offend other people with their personal views. Which usually helps in balancing the communication. Tipping the scale of balance in communication is a wrong move.

Few tips to become and inclusive communicator:

Understand the mindset of other people and value their perspective. You should understand that everyone has their own views of life and its problems. They may even have different ways of solving such problems. So forcing your perspective or solution to some problem onto someone is big no.

Don't state unnecessary characteristics of someone until needed.

For example, there is a person Alfred who happens to be fat and he is having to transfer to a different city. So you don't need to say it like " Alfred that fat one is transferring." Specifying his body feature here is totally unnecessary.

Do not assume a person's gender or sexuality. At any post any place any gender can work and they can have their own sexual preference. There is no rule that higher posts can only have straight male or something like that. So you are not allowed to assume just like that.

Disregard any stereotype. Any kind of stereotype may it be religion, race, caste etc is not a good norm of communication. It not only has an adverse affect on your communication with people but also adversely affects your character.

Show respect while regarding any person's race or ethnicity.

While regarding any person's disability do it in a neutral form so that they don't get hurt.

Don't categorise people on the basis of their disability. They should be known by themselves not by their disabilities.

There might be some instances where a person says something about them or someone close to them but they might get offended when it is said by a third person.

Do not patronize someone. Sometimes all you are showing is sympathy to someone but to them it's like patronizing. Like your praising them for existing, which is not a good thing.

Even jokingly try not to make any joke that can harm the mindset of other people.

You need to understand the mindset of all people and then communicate according to the level where they are offended. Not all people get offended easily while some get offended very quickly. You have to keep in mind their nature and then communicate.

Vocabulary

Another thing which can help you in communicating is improving your vocabulary. Sometimes what happens is there are two word for same meaning but one might be too harsh or sometimes not suitable in that situation. So by expanding your vocabulary you will have widen your choices of words. Then you will have full liberty of thinking which word will work the best in that situation and choose it. In this way your communication can go smoothly.

There are few ways to improve your vocabulary:

First is the most basic one, which is reading books. There you might encounter some words which you then check in the dictionary. In this way that word will get stored in your brain and your vocabulary will enhance further,

Using new words for the same terms in daily life. For example, using encounter word instead of meet.

Break down words and understand their meaning. By learning the meaning of their parts you will have a better understanding of the word and can use it in more better way.

Looking and Seeing

The concept of looking and seeing is quite similar to listening and hearing. Seeing is without observation i.e; not gathering all the information from the object where as looking is gathering every bit of information from the object, carefully observing and analysing it.

Looking can be quite helpful when we are talking about communication. Many times our body posture, eye focus and facial expression speaks more than our voice. Many psychologists are able to tell whether a person is lying or not just by looking at them talking. Therefore, looking is a very important aspect of communication.

Direct contact is one way to communicate in a better way. It shows the other person that we are interested in the conversation. It is also a sign of confidence.

At the beginning many people are nervous to make direct eye contact. They can take this entire process step wise.

Firstly, start by standing in front of a mirror and talking to yourself while making direct eye contact.

Secondly, start making conversation with someone very close to you while making direct eye contact, if that looks a bit tough then you can start by looking somewhere near to the eye avoiding direct eye contact and then move one to eye contact.

Thirdly, do the same with a distant relative.

And finally, do the same with complete strangers.

Doing these steps might take a lot of time maybe more than a month or so but eventually you will be able to make direct eye contact while holding a conversation with anyone.

ÞÞÞ

Self-Notes

4

Social Anxiety

We all know the feeling of being nervous or uncomfortable in a social situation. Maybe you've clammed up when meeting someone new or gotten sweaty palms before making a big presentation. Public speaking or walking into a roomful of strangers isn't exactly thrilling for everybody, but most people can get through it. This feeling is called social anxiety or social phobia. The stress of these situations is too much to handle. You might, for example, avoid all social contact because things that other people consider "normal" -- like making small talk and eye contact -- make you so uncomfortable. All aspects of your life, not just the social, could start to fall apart.

People having social anxiety may face:

1. *Talking to strangers*
2. *Speaking in public*
3. *Dating*
4. *Making eye contact*
5. *Entering rooms*
6. *Using public restrooms*
7. *Going to parties*
8. *Eating in front of other people*
9. *Going to school or work*
10. *Starting conversations*

Every person has a different level of social anxiety. For example, someone can be great in one-on-one conversation but might be afraid of groups.

In general, social anxiety is an overwhelming fear of:

1. *Being judged or watched by others in social situations*

2. *Being embarrassed or humiliated -- and showing it by blushing, sweating, or shaking*

3. *Accidentally offending someone*

4. *Being the center of attention*

5. *If you are in social anxiety you might feel:*

6. *Very self-conscious in social situations*

7.

A persistent, intense, and chronic fear of being judged by others

8. *Shy and uncomfortable when being watched (giving a presentation, talking in a group)*

9. *Hesitant to talk to others*

10. *The need to avoid eye contact*

11. *Rapid heartbeat*

12. *Muscle tension*

13. *Dizziness and lightheadedness*

14. *Blushing*

15. *Crying*

16. *Sweating*

17.

Stomach trouble and diarrhea

18. *Inability to catch breath*

19. *An "out-of-body" sensation*

Social anxiety can have many effect on you like:

1. *Low self-esteem*

2. *Negative thoughts*

3. *Depression*

4. *Sensitivity to criticism*

5. *Poor social skills that don't improve*

Walking up to a coworker, friend could feel like a nightmare coming true, but it doesn't have to be. Even in a completely empty room you are not alone. In social anxiety one even fears talking to oneself. Breaking the ice between themselves and talking is the first step to overcome social anxiety.Once a person takes a deeper look at themselves and their own needs, speaking up can become much easier.

Gaining social achievement both personally and professionally starts from one self. They need to dissect themselves and start analysing their personalities.Assessing personality can help someone learn where they can push themselves and where their absolute limits are. For example, introverts tend to thrive on quiet, alone time. They often need time to process the day and think through upcoming tasks. Knowing this, an introvert can limit their social exposure so they are never overworked when interacting with others. They can schedule times in the day to sit in quiet reflection and gather their thoughts before going back into the world. Extroverts, however, thrive on interacting with others. If they were stuck in the house alone all day, it would likely be a horrible day for them. Even extroverts who are timid in conversations can meet their social needs by going to public places. Sitting in a coffee shop or walking around a mall can simulate the interactive experience and might quell the extrovert's need for other people.

For people having social anxiety, a social gathering or something of the same sort can be a very uncomfortable place. People instinctively tend to do activities that will put them in a safe zone i.e; comfort zone.Therefore, people tend to avoid social interaction and avoid any gatherings possible. So in order to break this social anxiety one needs to consciously apply force and exit their comfort zone and after a certain amount of time their comfort zone will expand. Soon enough they will be able to communicate to a person without any problem. Repeating the same will allow them to be able to interact with smaller groups and then a larger group and then they might be able to even become a public speaker.

Staying in a comfort zone can lead to missing out on life experiences the person may enjoy if they can get past the initial shock. Someone who is afraid to travel may never leave their hometown if they choose not to push the boundaries of their safe space. This means they never see the world beyond the area where they grew up, which can amount to missed experiences and lessons not learned

To leave the comfort zone, people have to be willing to embrace the pain that comes with stepping outside of it. Many experiences beyond a comfort zone will register immediate panic or discomfort, but often times if someone sticks with the activity they are able to realize it is not as painful as they anticipated. Learning to embrace the pain means the person accepts that attempting something outside of their comfort zone may be difficult, but the experience is worth the challenge. Embracing the pain of the unknown leads to increased confidence and a sense of power. Once a person realizes they are able to overcome their fears, they can continue to do so throughout their life.

To leave the comfort zone, people have to be willing to embrace the pain that comes with stepping outside of it. Many experiences beyond a comfort zone will register immediate panic or discomfort, but often times if someone sticks with the activity they are able to realize it is not as painful as they anticipated. Learning to embrace the pain means the person accepts that attempting something outside of their comfort zone may be difficult, but the experience is worth the challenge. Embracing the pain of the unknown leads to increased confidence and a sense of power. Once a person realizes they are able to overcome their fears, they can continue to do so throughout their life.

A person can also replace self-deprecating thoughts with an argument for why the trait in question is desirable. For example, if someone has it in mind that their sense of humor is not widely appreciated, they could argue that more people wished they had a niche humor instead of the blanket jokes everyone has heard before. Turning a negative into a positive helps create an appreciation for the traits the person possesses. Therefore, embracing positivity can play a vital role in ending this social anxiety for good.

Challenge can be one effective way to end social anxiety. Like setting a goal to say "hello" to a total stranger or maybe talk 20 minutes to friend who hasn't been in contact for a long time. The human mind is made in such a way that it acts in its full potential when in a competitive mode. This is the reason that in every corner of the world no matter whatever field competitiveness is promoted on a wide scale.

Exposure therapy can help someone confront a scary situation and gradually become comfortable in it. The process is simple. A person will determine something that causes them anxiety or fear and begin exposing themselves to that thing in small doses. For example, if someone is afraid of snakes they might go to the zoo and look at the snake exhibit every day until they begin to feel more comfortable around them. The exercise should only be performed for as long as it takes the person to feel comfortable with the situation. The goal is to take less time getting comfortable at each exposure and build up a sort of tolerance to the situation. Over time, the person should be able to tolerate more and more time in the uncomfortable situation without intense levels of fear or anxiety. Eventually, the fear may disappear completely.

Surrounding oneself with people who have similar interests and goals also makes approaching those people easier. The common ground is a conversation-starter that has potential to lead elsewhere or just give someone practice interacting with different types of people. Interacting with people in a group can also lead to meeting new friends through networking. Groups are a great place to be introduced to new people and grow a personal social network. The more friends a person has the greater chance they will find someone they are comfortable sharing their opinions with.

ᕗᕗᕗ

Self-Notes

5

Feelings of Conversation

When one talks about coversation one needs to understand the importance of mood. The mood of the conversation should be according to the topic. Light mood for normal topics where as heavy mood for serious topics. Mismatching these would eventually lead to end of conversation. Either you or the other person or both would get the feeling of killing the conversation as soon as possible. Having a heavy mood for normal conversation will start feeling too intimidating. Whereas, if mood is too light for serious topic the conversation will becom joke. So appropriate mood is necessary. Generally, one needs to avoid being intimidating while interacting with strangers and try to preserve a light mood. One can do this will introducing laughing element in the conversation to lighten the mood. A small smile can proove to change the mood of conversation quickly.

We need to keep and open mind while communicating because this helps us in hearing different opinions. Sometimes people are met with ideas that are very different from their own and remaining open can be a challenge. it can be helpful to remember that the goal of a conversation is not to start an argument, but to collaborate with others and share ideas. The key to not responding negatively to new ideas is to keep emotions in check, stay present in the conversation, and don't be afraid to leave a comfort zone. Therefore, we can say that emotion play a vital role in communication.

Participating in small talk and starting a new conversation both depend on a certain lightheartedness from both parties to keep the mood positive. If someone dives into a heavy subject, it can kill the mood right away. Inversely, keeping things too light can sometimes lead to people thinking someone is not capable of serious discussion. There is a delicate middle ground people need to be able to tread to start quality conversations.

When trying to start a conversation with a new person, someone should not rely on opportunities to poke fun at the person as an opener. Someone might accidentally call out a quality the other person is sensitive to and does not want other people to notice. This can make them upset before the conversation even begins and not want to engage socially. Same this thing can happen to you but to have an excellent communicating skill means to avoid it. It doesnt mean that you don't need to get offended. It's okay to feel upset in such cases but the key to keep the conversation going is to not to let it bother you. Laugh at yourself so the conversation can continue and it does not become awkward for the other members.

While approaching a group it is advisable to start with light topics like one which can be common to everyone. This can include a common experience, the weather, the commute to work, or anything else that everyone is sure to have an opinion about.

Another way to approach a lighthearted conversation is to ask the other person about themselves. This gives the person the opportunity to decide the topic and tone of the conversation, which ensures their comfort. It is good to try to pick a context for a good introduction. Something which can be realted at that particular moment. For example, if a person is in bookstore then you can start by asking their review on a particular book or by asking their favourite books or authors.

The more good deeds a person does, the better sense of their own morality they have. Most people strive to be good people. They go out of their way to help others when they have the opportunity and they actively try to make others feel happy and accepted. Part of treating everyone with kindness might mean meeting new people along the way. Meeting new people means being exposed to new ideas and opinions.

When someone has ideas or opinions that don't match another person's, they should always approach the conversation with an open mind and do their best not to judge the other person. Part of interacting with new people is getting to know their viewpoint and background to better understand their perspective. This kind of approach in life is called learning approach.

No matter whether the person infront of you is younger or older than you, keeping the fact that you may learn something from them in mind will really help you in not only communication but in every aspect of life. A person with a learning attitude is whom we call a growing person. People can learn a great deal by discussing problems or topics with someone who has a different viewpoint than them. It can teach people to consider the opposite side of the argument and in some cases strengthen their beliefs. Some situations cause a change of heart when someone considers the opposing side of the issue, but others serve as proof as to why someone believes what they do. The most important step to learning from other people's perspective is to remember that an opinion is not correct just because someone has always held it. Remaining open to change and changing their mind can be the difference between learning and being obstinate.

Another thing you need to remember is laughing is the key to success. Not everyone is confident and not everyone is sure if they should point out their flaws or try to make sure no one notices. Despite what most people might think, making certain types of jokes at one's own expense actually signals confidence and self-assurance. It shows that a person is secure enough with their short-comings to put them on display for others. This confidence shows in the way they can point out a mistake or quirk and laugh along with the group at themselves. In fact, it has been found that people who utilize self-deprecating humor typically have higher mental scores. Thus, we can say that by laughing you not only help the conversation keep going but also show a better self-confidence. This is quite striking skill if you want to pursue marketing or management fields in future.

Sometimes going on a blind date can be especially awkward. The two people have never met, are not sure if they have any common interests, and have no idea what the other person's boundaries might be. The tactics can help smooth over a rough start by opening an easy conversation and keeping the humor consistent to ease tensions. If someone can also manage to be open minded, then the other person will probably be encouraged to speak more and keep the conversation moving.

Another very good way to keep the conversation moving in such scenarios are open ended question where the conversation can keep linking from one question to another and eventualy it can lead to a bigger easy conversation.

ÞÞÞ

Self-Notes

6

Appearance and Expressions

When someone is aware of their appearance they are able to manipulate it in their favor and present a calm, cool, and collected persona to others. Part of presenting this image, though, is believing in oneself and having the confidence to dress like an executive. Clothes play a large role in communicating and people can use them to show what mood there in and even what mood they'd like to be in. Most people dress according to mood, but dressing for mood someone else wants is not a good practice. People's posture and non-verbal cues can mean more to others than their words, so it is critical that they make sure the messages match. Finally, before initiating conversation one needs to be ready with all the tools like being open minded, respect of others opinion etc.

As we have already discussed in previous chapter that eyes also play an important role in communication. And the first things our eye notice is appearance. There's an old saying that " First impression is the last impression". While there are many things to consider in first impression like appearance, language, behaviour etc. But appearance plays a major role in the first impression that any person perceives of us. So we need to keep in mind to balance our appearance. By balancing we mean that we need to maintain the appearance such that the conversation doesn't loose it's value. For example, suppose there is a meeting with some client of yours and that matter is quite official and serious and you meet theme dressed funky, at that immidiate moment the conversation will loose it's value since the client will start having doubt about how much importance you are giving. Similarly, if you dressed like meeting in a party then the meaning of party to relax and enjoy will be lost. So maintaining the balance is the real key in standing out in a good way.

In interpersonal communication, the appearance of the participants establishes their social identity. By our appearance cues, we often send messages designed to construct a social reality or social identity for ourselves that we could not and would not want to construct by verbal means (Kaiser, 1990). Thus, the judicious person will not say to another person, "I am trying to impress you" or "I am trying to dominate you," but the same person will routinely and repeatedly communicate such messages visually by the kinds of clothing he or she chooses to wear.

You should ensure that you are appropriately groomed. This does not mean that women have to spend two hours putting on make-up before attending an event. It does, however, mean that you should be clean, your clothes should be clean and ironed, and that your hair should be tidy.

Nobody expects you to be packaged into something you are not. However, your appearance is a reflection of your own self-esteem. You should aim to present yourself to your best possible advantage. Whilst you might be casually dressed when working within your organisation, a more formal approach may well be preferable when representing your organisation at an external meeting.

Good grooming and a tidy appearance is always preferable, whether casually or more formally dressed. It presents a much more professional appearance.

It also suggests that you think that you are relatively important: that you matter. This is important if you wish to be taken seriously. Nobody is going to respect someone who does not look like they respect themselves.

One of the reasons that people often complain about telephone and email, not to mention social media, is that they do not allow for any non-verbal communication. This means that a huge part of meaning can be lost.

On the telephone, for instance, you have to work much harder on conveying your emotional response with your voice, because your face is not visible.

In email and social media, we have adopted 'emojis' or emoticons to express our emotions.Little can be done to alter your face, but a lot can be done about the expression that is on it!

It does not matter how the day started or what minor crisis has occurred along the way. People have not come to this event or meeting to see you looking gloomy. If you do not look interested and enthusiastic about what you are saying, why should anyone else care?

It is your duty—to yourself as well as to the organisation that you represent—to convey a calm, friendly and professional exterior, whatever you may feel inside. Try to smile and appear optimistic and confident. More to the point, try to convey how you (should) feel about a subject in which you are an expert: at least interested and capable, and preferably enthusiastic.

Paradoxically, simply behaving as though you are confident can actually help you to become more confident. This is very much a 'virtuous circle'.

Scientists have found that there may be a biological basis to the importance of eye contact in human communication. A study published in 2007 found that certain iris characteristics, and in particular the way in which the lines radiate out from the centre, and curve around the outer edge, were associated with certain personality traits. This may sound like eugenics, but the study's authors speculated that the results might be due to the same gene being responsible for development of both the iris and the frontal cortex in the brain, which is the area linked to personality. This sounds feasible, but clearly needs a lot more work before it is accepted.

It does, however, offer a possible clue as to why we value being able to make steady eye contact when we speak to someone else.

Para-language relates to all aspects of the voice which are not strictly part of the verbal message, including the tone and pitch of the voice, the speed and volume at which a message is delivered, and pauses and hesitations between words.

Emphasising particular words, or the use of particular tones of voice can imply whether or not feedback is required. For example, in English, and other non-tonal languages, a rising tone at the end of the sentence can indicate a question.

So we need to keep in mind that appearance, facial expression and para-language plays and important role in communication as non-verbal part of it.

ÞÞÞ

Self-Notes

7

Things to Remember

In the end there are few things to keep in mind.

Listening

As we have already discussed that how being a good listener is a crucial part of good communication skills.

Now, here are few tips on how to be a good listener:

- *When you are listening give your full attention to the speaker*

-

If you have a phone , be sure to set its face down.

- *If you are working on computer then turn away from it to show your interest .*

- *Look at their non-verbal signals , and listen to their words.*

- *Use clarification questions to follow up on key points and then sum up your understanding to them , so they can clear up any miscommunication immediately*

- *Notice whether the person is making direct eye contact or not.*

- *Look for the comfort zone of other person.*

Non-verbal

To begin improving your non-verbal communication, first, you must begin by paying attention to it.

OBSERVE YOURSELF

- *Do you make consistent eye contact?*
- *How do you position yourself when speaking to people ?*
- *Does it change based on who you are talking to?*
- *How do people react to you?*

OBSERVE OTHERS

- *Are there certain people who make you feel heard?*
- *What do they do that makes you feel like that?*
-

Is there someone who is unpleasant to communicate with?

- *Why?*

- *What actions do they do that make you not enjoy talking to them?*

- *Think about the positives and negatives that you observe.*

How to be good at non-verbal communication

- *Don't fidget! This is rule number one. Be still, and calm. This communicates that you are in control, confident and a force to be reckoned with.*

- *Use eye contact intelligently. Focus in on people when you want to drive home a point. Look people in the eye both when you are listening to them and when you are speaking.*

-

Be confident in your use of space. Don't minimize yourself, instead relax into your space. It's important that you do this intelligently! Don't prevent other people from sitting comfortably.

- *Strive to be non-reactive during stressful situations. Keep your emotions level and respond calmly.*

- *Simply being more aware of non-verbal communication, and the power that it has will help you be better at using it proactively and positively.*

Verbal Communication

To improve your verbal communication, you'll need to get better at both what you say and how you say it.

OBSERVE YOURSELF

- *How do people react to you?*

- *Are there times when they react more negatively than others, and can you pinpoint why?*

- *Are there colleagues who you particularly enjoy conversing with?*

- *Why?*

- *Observe how communication happens in your work environment, and pay attention to which aspects are positive and negative.*

Before you speak, know what you want to communicate.

- *Begin with your stated purpose ('I think we need to increase ad spending 10%')*

- *Move on to your reasoning ('The upcoming holiday season is a prime time to target our customers more effectively')*

-

Review possible outcomes ('We could increase sales between 20 and 30%').

•

Use pitch to help captivate your audience

•

A lower pitch tends to communicate gravitas and experience. Take longer, deeper breaths and speak from your diaphragm to lower your voice.

•

Strategically use silence to capture, and keep attention. Pause and hook the viewer's attention before dropping your pitch, your big reveal or your thesis sentence.

•

Use a range of cadence, speed and style. You don't want to speak in a monotone, you'll bore your audience and they won't be engaged in the content of your communication.

WRITTEN COMMUNICATION

In written communication, the first step to improve is to make sure that your spelling and grammar are perfect.

- *Take the time to re-read everything that you write*
- *Is your tone appropriate to the setting?*
- *Are there any mistakes, items not linked properly, or missing points?*
- *Have you covered the subject in enough depth?*
- *We often overestimate how much other people know about our specialist subjects, it might be necessary to write in more detail. At the same time, don't write a novel!*

Formatting is key

- *Format everything, from a Slack message to a full presentation, to make sure that you are creating a readable text.*
- *Use bullet points and paragraphs to break up your message.*
- *Highlight your points in bold if you have a lot of text.*
- *Underline anything that you think is crucial.*

More tips for improving your written communication:

- *State your assumptions. This will help avoid miscommunications. Start by saying 'I assume you have heard about the new policy change, effective June 1. Because of this, we will be adjusting x, y and z.*
-

'Read often. From messages to novels, read often and when you do, think about what you like (or dislike) about what you're reading. Emulate what you like, and work to avoid what you dislike.

- *Use framing to get your point across. Think about it from the recipient's point of view, and what's in it for them, and then frame the message to highlight that.*

- *Read your writing out loud to check for mistakes. Use this time to review grammar, tone, fact-check and to make sure that you have covered everything you wanted to in the communication.*

- *When possible, use clear examples and avoid using too much jargon.*

VISUAL COMMUNICATION

An important aspect of using visual communication is to only use it when necessary.

Tips for improving visual communication:

- *Less is more! Pare back your design and resist the urge to stuff every fact, figure, font and color into a presentation.*

- *Utilize typography. If in doubt, ask for the brand guidelines for your company and follow those. They will help you create cohesive presentations in line with your company's preferred look.*

- *Pay attention to balance and harmony. You can achieve this by using similar, rather than disparate, elements in your communication. The same style of clip art, the same font family, or the same pastel shades.*

- *Begin with the end in mind. Know what you want to communicate and start there.*

CLARITY AND CONCISION

Good verbal communication means saying just enough—don't talk too much or too little. Try to convey your message in as few words as possible. Say what you want clearly and directly, whether you're speaking to someone in person, on the phone, or via email. If you ramble on, your listener will either tune you out or will be unsure of exactly what you want.

FRIENDLINESS

Through a friendly tone, a personal question, or simply a smile, you will encourage your co-workers to engage in open and honest communication with you. It's important to be polite in all your workplace communications.

This is important in both face-to-face and written communication. When you can, personalize your emails to co-workers and/or employees – a quick "I hope you all had a good weekend" at the start of an email can personalize a message and make the recipient feel more appreciated.

CONFIDENCE

It is important to be confident in your interactions with others. Confidence shows your co-workers that you believe in what you're saying and will follow through.

Exuding confidence can be as simple as making eye contact or using a firm but friendly tone. Avoid making statements sound like questions. Of course, be careful not to sound arrogant or aggressive. Be sure you are always listening to and empathizing with the other person.

EMPATHY

Using phrases as simple as "I understand where you are coming from" demonstrates that you have been listening to the other person and respect their opinions. Active listening can help you tune in to what your conversational partner is thinking and feeling, which will, in turn, make it easier to display empathy.

OPEN-MINDED

A good communicator should enter into any conversation with a flexible, open mind. Be open to listening to and understanding the other person's point of view, rather than simply getting your message across.

By being willing to enter into a dialogue, even with people with whom you disagree, you will be able to have more honest, productive

RESPECT

People will be more open to communicating with you if you convey respect for them and their ideas. Simple actions like using a person's name, making eye contact, and actively listening when a person speaks will make the person feel appreciated. On the phone, avoid distractions and stay focused on the conversation.

Convey respect through email by taking the time to edit your message. If you send a sloppily written, confusing email, the recipient will think that you do not respect her enough to think through your communication with her.

FEEDBACK

Being able to give and receive feedback appropriately is an important communication skill. Managers and supervisors should continuously look for ways to provide employees with constructive feedback, be it through email, phone calls, or weekly status updates.

Similarly, you should be able to accept and even encourage feedback from others. Listen to the feedback you are given, ask clarifying questions if you are unsure of the issue, and make efforts to implement the feedback.

MEDIUM

An important communication skill is to simply know what form of communication to use. For example, some serious conversations (layoffs, resignation, changes in salary, etc.) are almost always best done in person.

You should also think about the person with whom you wish to speak. If they are a very busy person (such as your boss, perhaps), you might want to convey your message through email. People will appreciate your thoughtful means of communication and will be more likely to respond positively to you.

Self-Notes

9 798887 838229

Printed by Libri Plureos GmbH in Hamburg, Germany